Rocking CHAIR
Reflections

Robert Scott

Published in Australia by Sid Harta Books & Print Pty Ltd,
ABN: 34632585293
23 Stirling Crescent, Glen Waverley, Victoria 3150 Australia
Telephone: +61 3 9560 9920, Facsimile: +61 3 9545 1742
E-mail: author@sidharta.com.au

First published in Australia 2022
This edition published 2022
Copyright © Robert Scott 2022
Cover design, typesetting: WorkingType (www.workingtype.com.au)

The right of Robert Scott to be identified as the Author of the Work
has been asserted in accordance with the Copyright, Designs and Patents Act 1988.

All rights reserved. No part of this publication may be reproduced,
stored in a retrieval system, or transmitted, in any form or by any means without the prior
written permission of the publisher, nor be otherwise circulated in any form of binding or
cover other than that in which it is published and without a similar condition being imposed on
the subsequent purchaser.

Robert Scott
Rocking Chair Reflections
ISBN: 978-1-925707-95-3
pp 132

Robert Scott was born and raised in England. He did his military service in Cyprus and migrated to Australia while still in his twenties. Between many jobs, he engaged in a lot of shoestring-budget travelling, including long overland trips (Sydney to London and England to India et cetera).

Now that Robert is seriously middle-aged and spectacularly poor, he travels mainly in his mind. He lives in Sydney.

Previously published by this author:
Mixed memories in my mind

With love to Joan, Dave, Rita and Peter and profound gratitude to ever helpful friend, Adrian Wootton.

Contents

About the Author	iii
Introduction	1
Cricket	3
Samaritan	5
Blessed Day	7
A Matter of Age	9
Age-Care Nursing	11
Behind the Hill	13
Belief	15
Best and Only Man	17
Caught in the System	19
Change Needed	22
Changed Perspective	24
Climate Change	26
Compassion	28
'Death' – Consolation	30
Digital-Dunce	32
Escape	34
Gratitude	36
Faith	38

First Flight	40
Focus	42
Gambler	44
A First Touch of Reality (Gap-Year)	46
Ghost writer	48
Homeless	50
Hopes	52
H.S.C.	54
In Praise of Trees	56
Is Birthright Right?	58
Just Kidding	60
Location Rules	62
Luck?	64
My Message	66
One Way	67
Perceptions	69
Life In Spirit (Perhaps)	71
Respect	73
The Pimple	75
The Power	78
Politics	80
Pressing On	82
Putting It Politely	84
Rain	86
Seeking the Way	88
Sleep	90
The Blessing	92
The Brother	95

The Decline	97
The Dilemma	99
The Journey	101
The Prayer	103
The Search	106
The Separation	108
The Weekend	110
Thought Control	112
Assisted Voluntary-Euthanasia	114
Winter Wine	116
Don't Walk Away	118
Aspects of Ageing	120
The Bridge	122

Introduction

Hi! I'm Bob Scott. I'm eighty-four at the time of publication. The 'About the Author' photograph shows me at the tender age of eighty-two.

For many years, I spent time in different countries, had many jobs and made long, overland trips. One of my hobbies was writing poems. In 2008, a book of my earlier poems was successfully published in England.

I generally use tradition-rhyming-verse since it remains enjoyable to most people.

Thank you for buying this book. I hope you enjoy it.

Robert Scott

Cricket

All morning-shopping has been done and everything seems well,
I need to know how runs stacked up, if any wickets fell.
My armchair is seductive; cricket's what this day's about,
The only worry comes in clouds, the dread of play washed out.

But then I'd doze, and dreams revert me to age-eight
in England, watching cricket without paying at the gate.
We had a well-worn system to follow every match,
having easily established a well-protected personal patch.

Our needs were neatly serviced by adjacent public field,
with solid corner-toilet-block, convenient to yield
a firm flat-roof next to the fence across which we could view
the cricket-field for free, without a payment due.

Friend-Ali was committed, an addicted, score-card king
and to his treasured notepad he was always poised to bring,
rapt record of each ball bowled, and also every run,
while I invented commentary, contributing cute fun.

'Lindwall's building his approach, now hitting his top gear,
his tools comprise hostility, ferocity and fear;
but, on release, his body sags, his anguish exposed raw,
as Compton sways aside and calmly cuts the ball for four.'

In post-war childhood spent upon that north-east coast,
of every sport, I seemed consumed by cricket most.
While winter-seasons intervened, with soccer 'all the rage',
how well it all now serves my advanced age.

Home is now Australia, my base for fifty years,
and life has produced so many smiles and sometimes many tears.
Now, in my Bondi-unit, I prepare to settle down,
my headphones hooked around my head and firm upon my crown.

*

First 'Ashes'-test is underway, my loyalties much mixed;
my English-roots still play a part, if not so firmly fixed.
My Aussie-sentiments still strong as telly is switched on,
while England-wins are welcome, Steve Smith can score his 'ton'.

I'm now perceived as 'oldie'; I know Ali's 'passed away',
but while I'm watching cricket, memory also tends to stray.
His concentration was intense upon his lasting score-card proof,
and cricket's reconnecting us, upon that toilet-roof.

Samaritan

I often muse, in wonder, at my path to this late stage,
with many twists and turns in passing eighty-years of age;
and as I pause to ponder distant childhood and my youth
in north-east England, at *ease* with post-war poverty, in truth.

I'm well aware, in memory's dream, of order that prevailed,
of accent and appearance that membership entailed;
that non-conformity to these conspired to exclude,
and caused some separation based *not* on mind or mood.

An example of 'not-fitting' was a family of Jews,
in apparent isolation, we accepted without views.
A teenager, much scorned, who seemed so banished and 'at-bay',
back then more harshly labelled than by euphemistic 'gay'.

On leaving school, my test could be a lone *weekend* not lost;
I had rail-fares, but not the means to cover hotel-cost.
Friend's older-brother would *take* me to his home in Kensal-Rise,
from London, twenty miles by train; I wasn't 'travel-wise'.

*

I was testing independence prior *to* my search for work;
I'd never wandered far from home, felt apprehension lurk
through seven hours, London-bound, along the railway-track;
so much time to contemplate, no means of turning back.

Released at Kings Cross station in*to* the bustling throng,
I felt a bit bewildered with no place to which belong;
no comforting familiar-face, no compass to consult,
help needed for direction, no known *outcome* or result.

Darkness had descended and exhaustion fogged my mind;
I knew by then I'd missed last train, this body left behind.
I came across a street bench where I waited for despair;
but strange *calm*ness crept upon me to incline me not to care,

*

and sure enough a car pulled up, a stranger to approach;
to check on me and my sad tale, perhaps some pity poach.
'Hop in my car,' said he. 'Fear *not*, I'll take you there.'
Somehow, I simply trusted him; could take me anywhere.

Long drive to find the suburb, the street and then the gate;
He waved away my meagre cash, was still prepared to wait.
I found my tongue to thank him and I need no coin to spin,
I chose to seek his level by embracing his black skin.

Blessed Day

I woke this morning feeling good,
with sleep producing a mellow mood
in which I embraced the day ahead;
and even more, once washed and fed.

I offered thanks for health intact,
for friends with whom to interact
and weather that was kind and calm;
no aspect that could cause alarm,

free from anxiety or stress,
at peace within the day's caress;
so grateful still to be alive
and free from goals for which to strive,

and from demands to be fulfilled,
or sense-of-urgency-instilled;
no target that needs to be achieved,
no pressure still to be relieved.

No irksome burden on my back
and nothing needed that I lack;
the day could not be more complete,
with sun-spread warmth to bathe my street.

Retired now, no duty calls,
no single chore my mind recalls;
for Nature's riches all around
I feel a love that's quite profound.

So many blessings offered free,
like chirping birds in leaf-clad tree;
and such *relief* rely upon—
all trace of toothache now quite gone.

A Matter of Age

Sam's struggling with the day ahead,
as with the day before;
Not much happening in his head
seems clear any more.

When he rises in the morning,
there's a film of mental-fog
that defies an early dawning,
while his brain seems in a bog.

It takes so long to pee as well,
and whinging would be sadder;
for many have worse tales to tell
than a slow-delivering bladder,

or even hair that never grows,
no more a source of pride;
and glasses, misplaced on his nose,
make hair-loss hard to hide.

There is a shuffle in his walk,
his teeth seem slightly slack;
he'd hate to hit a need to talk,
his thinking is off-track.

Outside, he needs his walking-frame,
more time to reach his club;
but distance-covered stays the same
and aches could use a rub.

The bloody key seems lost again,
he's scrambled round the floor
and now he sees—is nothing sane?
It's sticking in the door.

He thinks he's dying every day,
if he's just caught a cold;
yet, not that simple Sam, they *say*,
just sadly growing old.

Age-Care Nursing

So many tasks must load the day,
some raising hope and some dismay;
remake all beds and launder sheets,
so subject-to-routine repeats.

Cut the toenails, bathe the feet,
such needs are never quite complete;
apply a bandage to an arm
with care to keep the patient calm,

help to prop her up in bed
to change the band-aid on her head;
and very gently comb her hair
and sweetly smile that sign-of-care,

then take around the coffee-jug,
a dainty cup, a treasured mug;
while taking time to re-assure,
concerned to *comfort if* not cure,

compelled to keep all dry and warm,
fixed times for functions to conform;
involvement and engagement sought,
providing meaning and support.

That gentle hand to guide a walk,
some precious moment just to talk;
thoughts of notes to be compiled
and issues to be *re*conciled.

Some patients wail, though not in pain,
and some who suffer don't complain;
sometimes tight lips and icy glare—
or faces friendly and aware.

For some, an end is very close,
perhaps one final pill or dose;
with *some* recoiling from Death's face—
more go with dignity and grace.

Behind the Hill

Untimely urge to overtake
the sudden stamping on a brake;
a surging screech from cars behind,
the crunch to which Fate seems inclined.

While off the road, beyond a hill,
there lies a lake, so deep and still,
where birds converge to meet-and-tweet,
or nestle on the water-sheet.

Around the lake, peace undisturbed,
swans glide serenely, unperturbed,
on silky surface, in sweet air,
calm and content, quite free from care.

There's havoc on the highway where collision has occurred,
skewed cars with occupants entrapped by injuries incurred;
unable to extract themselves or ease relentless pain,
with slightly stifled screams for help or folded-facial strain.

Some victims will heal well enough to drive this road again,
resume the path of human-life in sunshine or in rain;
while others, not so lucky, have strong suffering to face,
and some may pass beyond the known to seek some better place.

A placid lake will welcome all without a single test,
surrounded by a lush green space inviting all to rest
beneath the many sturdy trees with foliage wide-spread,
on mats of softly-sinking grass with flowers at the head.

Belief

How tight the net our cultures weave
to then entrap what-to-believe;
to bury concepts, without grief,
that knowledge should outrank belief.

Religions can then best provide
a set of rules to which abide;
instil a sense of right-and-wrong,
protect the weak, restrict the strong,

for such provisions must prevail,
with wide awareness to entail;
if stable nations are to form
with laws to which all *must* conform.

And into groups we must submit,
embrace some wider role-to-fit;
while still retaining need to feel
some separate spark still strong and real,

some 'sense' on which we may rely,
of 'self' with which identify;
for separation still to strive
to keep that sense-of-self alive

and, too, a basic urge persists,
to know how everything exists;
elusive knowledge, it so seems,
resistant even in our dreams.

Perhaps the best approach may be,
in calm or sometimes-stormy sea;
to treat belief as hand-to-clasp,
'God-knowledge' quite beyond our grasp.

Concepts of 'God' seem ill-defined
to man-made images confined;
belief alone can be attained
if always nourished and sustained.

Deprived of knowing how-or-why,
no founder's-face sketched in the sky;
with love-and-care as seeds to sow,
Benign-belief will watch us grow.

Best and Only Man

In truth, I feel a little shy,
but, with your sympathy, I will try
to now perform, as well I can,
my role as best but *only* man,

a male who seems quite out of place,
a statue in a swimming-race;
just feeling like a limp excuse,
equipped with parts of little use.

But none of us has any choice,
in genes and gender should rejoice;
and love should blossom, unrestrained,
with life-fulfilment thus attained,

however programmed we may be,
our love unveiled for all to see,
confronting prejudice of some
with ignorance to overcome,

and so I hope to play my part
and hail this union from its start
and bless the bride, and bless the bride
in marriage born of love and pride.

Caught in the System

I never could have pictured, even in my wildest dreams,
even fanned by fascination of all Fate's cruellest schemes;
so far beyond reflections of life's future turns and twists,
with chains around my ankles and handcuffs on my wrists.

Some unknown killer lurks in parks or hides himself inside,
but if he dabbles in disguise, no need for him to hide;
he doesn't *need* to look like me, with features much like mine,
as he appeared at the crime, by birth or by design,

enough to prove me guilty to this jury of my peers,
identified by witnesses infested by their fears.
I'd spent the testing-time alone, no alibi at hand;
could not explain my state-of-mind to make them understand

that I suffered from depression, hidden from general view,
was crushed by this occurrence, not expressing what was true,
with inclination to retreat into defensive-shell,
failing to articulate that truth I had to tell.

My struggle and my anguish seemed suggestive of my guilt,
with jury-members scowling as my agitation built.
Provided with a lawyer with a formal attitude
and reluctance to involve me that was close to being rude.

She stressed my instability in sticking to a job,
and friction in my family that made me want to sob,
and sought to paint a picture of some broken-life I led,
implying blame lay not with *me*, but circumstance instead

Her manner made me guilty, culpability-reduced,
and blame to be diluted by excuses introduced.
Her concept of defending me caused any hope to shred,
of any court that could accept my innocence instead.

Deliverer stood sternly for the verdict to proclaim,
to formalise and seal my guilt, solidify my shame.
Hostility heaved at the air to spread around the court,
as I panicked at the prospect of my sorry-life cut short.

But then there was commotion and new urgency arrived,
producing huddles round the judge, who then for order strived
by rapping with aggression until silence was restored;
'New information indicates the verdict fully flawed.

All charges hereby dismissed, the jury not in need.'
Officers directed that defendant now be freed,
with nothing now to answer, on character no stain;
the stain had only scarred my *soul*; heart heavy, still, with pain.

Clouded in confusion, I was bustled from that place.
Reporters pooled around me, of a friend there was no trace.
I belatedly discovered a new killing had occurred,
with DNA-link to the first–and all that it incurred.

Change Needed

When birds burst into morning-song,
it bids me to embrace; belong.
My mind maps out the day ahead,
prepares for rising from my bed.

Adjust my dress with fingers fumbling;
first steps unsteady, slightly stumbling,
with bladder begging for relief;
wash-basin, where the wipe is brief.

Half-hearted hassling with my hair,
comb-over calmer, with more care.
First food, with second coffee poured,
my brain and body half-restored.

Perhaps a shower and a shave;
elusive still, that look I crave.
Would women sense my urge to please
and pause to put me at my ease?

No chance of that, or so it seems;
they dally only in my dreams.
Or I'm deluded; don't deserve
an image proudly to preserve.

I double up on eggs-and-toast;
I still have intact-teeth to boast.
From 'fast-food' why need I refrain?
I'll back my belt to take the strain.

I think, perhaps, I'll 'make my peace';
my envy of Brad Pitt can cease.
Why sacrifice some dish or drink
in worship of some waistline-shrink?

*

I just won't worry how I look;
buy burgers and decline to cook;
no longer fuss or fret my hair,
but flop around, with flesh to spare.

In fact, I'm now inclined to slouch,
enjoy my evenings on the couch.
I should have thought of this before—
this line I'll draw at eighty-four.

Changed Perspective

My mind may dwell, in memory-float,
youth-years in England, now remote;
a lucky-land when I grew up,
with Wimbledon and F.A.-Cup.

There was one aspect of my youth
unwelcome, if I tell the truth,
as national-service was imposed,
ordeals to which we were exposed.

What most endures in my mind,
for which warm words are hard to find,
is basic-training for ten weeks—
a form of torture no-one seeks.

Obscenities spat in your face,
fuelled by derision and disgrace;
with curses that you have to wear,
indignities you're forced to bear,

with days of drilling on the square
and foul-mouthed corporals everywhere;
with guard-duty on icy nights,
for tingling-teeth and air that bites,

or wakened rudely, deep at night,
a fumbling, stumbling sorry-sight;
in bitter cold, all dreams betrayed,
outside, assembled, on-parade.

Queued up for pittance-pay doled out,
slum-slaves at whom to scream and shout;
cheap-labour for the army's use,
entrapped in legalised abuse

or so, it seemed to us back then
but yet, today, as ageing men,
most might well *reverse* those views
in answer to street-violence news.

Tough treatment, now far in the past,
instilled a discipline-to-last
that *strengthens*, rather than *erodes*,
all that protects communal-codes;
and could cause chaos to retreat—
return calm order to each street.

Climate Change

No shortage of dissent exists,
self-serving interest still persists
from most denying climate-change,
with firm resistance to arrange.

And stance as stubborn as a mule,
to block release from fossil-fuel.
Disaster may well loom ahead
once basic common-sense has fled.

Deniers must be met by mirth
as new proponents of 'flat-earth',
attempting to dispel unease
as melting icebergs swell the seas.

States Stephen Hawking's 'final bow';
Within a thousand-years from now,
without huge change, for what it's worth,
mankind will *be* wiped *off* the Earth.

Debate will battle to by-pass
the known effects of greenhouse-gas;
or mass-emissions caused by coal,
with deadly damage by 'own-goal'.

The sticking-point none can ignore,
competing-counter at the core;
all nations need secure supply
of power on which all rely.

Of course, the problem is world-wide,
solution needs all to abide
by measures nations *must* adopt;
no easy paths for which to opt.

And global-pressure must increase,
procrastination needs to cease;
with attitudes much re-arranged,
no generation left 'short-changed'.

All efforts must intensify,
creating new means of supply;
with lasting law and rigid rule
to phase out use of fossil-fuel.

Compassion

Probably, for most of us, perceptions are installed,
contained within preserved 'backyards' where boundaries are walled.
Could we cast aside all cliches and suspend all platitudes,
explore our blocked-in broad beliefs, review our attitudes?

Acknowledge, if not dwell-upon, our every flaw and failing,
extend such focus, round the world, to all those weak-and-wailing,
and contemplate the suffering, of others, far and wide,
and concentrate upon such fates from which we tend to hide?

Is fortune an entitlement that proves our human-worth,
or merely a reflection of 'kind-cards' dealt out at birth;
so each impoverished, ailing child, so fragile and forlorn,
is not some lesser-being just because of where she's born,

perhaps in weeping, war-torn land, where suffering is rife,
no law-and-order to protect, or provide peaceful life,
her home a mud-made shanty and her privacy unknown,
and where disease is rampant and no pity ever shown.

If fortune smiles upon us and we're in a happy place,
such privilege we should preserve, all aspects to embrace;
but still stay aware and caring for those so steeped in pain,
for compassion is the essence by which our souls sustain.

Some higher-power is in play, as 'Creation' must insist,
but a so-inept perspective provides little to assist;
no understanding that extends, beyond our human-scope,
to what it means or how it works, what purpose and what hope.

Hindu-sages have advised that 'karma' is the key,
reincarnation rotates births by selectivity
based upon lives-lived-before, by 'merit' gained from those,
if selfless caring and concern were options that we chose.

A human-birth provides a path to spiritually-evolve
with obstacles to overcome and issues to resolve;
detaching from self-interest and serving others first
and reaching for an advanced stage when service is a 'thirst'.

The nurses of our nations set the standards we might meet,
perhaps provide contentment and a peace that's quite complete.
If we could rank the virtues by the values that they bring,
caring, then, could be our queen, compassion could be king.

'Death' - Consolation

'Death' is the leveller, for all
of human-issues, large and small
by which are measured or perceived,
how much or little we've achieved.

However human-life proceeds,
whatever 'fails' or what 'succeeds';
eventually a line is drawn
beyond which waits a different dawn.

Be one revered or reviled,
as an adult *or* a child;
on *each* of us, time takes its toll
of brain and body, but not soul.

All inclination to compare,
with satisfaction or despair,
concepts of 'status' or of worth,
ends up as dust, returned to earth.

No human-form escapes this fate,
despite perceptions we create,
regardless of the lives we lead,
from luxury to abject need.

Each body has a 'use-by date'
and functions of the brain deflate.
By this, equality is spread,
no-one behind, no-one ahead.

None can repair or can retrieve
the human-life we're forced to leave,
and 'status' ceases to exist
where no misfortune can persist.

Death of the body and the brain
will end all suffering and pain
and, in addition, it will yield
for all, a level playing-field.

Digital-Dunce

I've noticed that the world has changed and I've been left behind.
It's just an observation and I have no 'axe-to-grind'.
I don't engage in gadgetry, don't own a mobile phone;
with humble land-line service, I'm content to live alone.

Pleased to pursue my human-path and grateful for good health,
but feel distinctly disinclined to worship worldly-wealth;
for riches swim within the heart, and in the mind as well,
with awakening-awareness of a dream on which to dwell.

Life's not a competition, or it doesn't need to be,
no rush to reach a corner if embracing what we see;
and age brings consolations in so many different ways,
with health, more freedom to be found, and less demanding days.

I treasure time with those-I-know who offer warmth and care,
but also to relax alone, to simply sit and stare
in peace, with people bustling-by, intent upon their needs,
while I reflect or recollect, while wondering where life leads.

Being active is required, but in ways we can select,
and we must indulge our interests to feed our intellect,
but, free from any fixed demands, we have the right of choice
to flow with what provides us with some reasons to rejoice.

So being eighty can be good if health remains intact,
and we welcome human-contact and take care to interact.
It doesn't need a laptop or a 'lifeline' mobile-phone,
or addiction to group-texting like dogs *worry*ing a bone.

There is no law preventing us from chatting on the street.
We can still *use* a land-line phone, and even sometimes meet.
If such crude-communication should ever fully fail,
we can buy a dollar-biro and resort to postal-mail.

I don't use credit cards at all, and can survive with cash,
and even in a bank-branch never break out in a rash.
I don't need endless photographs, and telly covers sport,
but technology eludes me, so I'd better act distraught.

Escape

Lost youth, reluctantly recalled,
suggests some need of noise installed,
when smoked-filled pubs, so packed with teens,
would bash our brains by many means,

by jukebox, or perhaps a band,
with blasting noise to rock the land,
all conversation crushed and killed,
drowned-out, destroyed, dismissed and stilled.

Noise still a drug, or so it seems,
for muddled moviemakers' dreams.
No movie scene can be complete
without mood-music or some beat.

Unfazed by bullets in his brain,
Clint tracks the villain like a train
through savage storm or sizzling heat,
pursued by ever-present beat.

From which we can emerge prepared
for drilling as the road's repaired;
then home-bound past the building-sites
for skyscrapers of breathless heights.
*

Perceptions now subdued by age,
with life played on a different stage;
I search for peace that calmness brings,
soothed by some song that silence sings,

seek sounds of Nature to appease,
birdcalls to comfort and to please;
rippling water, rustling leaves,
sound that relaxes and relieves.

Some rural-retreat I must find,
where peace prevails, with people kind;
where men don't feel the need to shout,
nor women scream all greetings out;

and traffic is more dignified
and simple life is signified;
with space to spare and people, aged,
escaping lives where chaos raged.

Gratitude

Few pursue a path so long
to find a place where all belong,
in search of Source from which we come
based on belief, abused by some.

Most settle for this human-form,
our fate in calmness or in storm;
where self-survival seems supreme,
not searching for elusive dream.

Survival asks that all compete
for human-comforts quite complete,
at highest levels in all ways
as signs that our 'success' displays.

But many find 'success' obscure,
sense failure and feel insecure;
and potholes on this human-road
can cause commitment to erode.

Some suffer from unhelpful birth
that is not blessed by wealth-and-worth,
but disadvantaged from the start,
denied such privilege, set apart.

Can luckless-birth be overcome,
or prove intense and troublesome,
with expectation then set low,
suppressing hope, obstructing flow?

Australia is a so-blessed land,
such scope for fortune to expand,
permitting effort to succeed,
providing help for all in need.

If to compare we feel compelled,
a wide perspective should be held,
including each impoverished land
with plights our pity must demand.

We need awareness, to apply,
of all that serves to satisfy;
sometimes amending attitude
to love this land, with gratitude.

Faith

Religions serve some 'Being' as creator of all known,
beyond our comprehension and requiring faith alone;
though many claim 'awakenings', with higher forms revealed
as focus for our worship that was previously concealed.

We can accept, without a way to clearly connect,
a 'Source' of our existence too elusive to inspect.
We also can assume such 'Source' asserting full control,
with purpose to protect us like some sentry on patrol.

With faith, no knowledge will we need,
confronting 'storms' with little heed.
Faith can protect, and needs no proof,
and will provide with 'walls' and 'roof'.

Securing us in times of strife,
or sickness, through our human-life;
for faith can cause us to keep calm
and to proceed, free from alarm.

For faith reaps reassurance in dealing with demands,
deflating daily pressures as our confidence expands,
unless disaster could cause doubt that faith may be misplaced
in whom to be directed, or on what it may be based.

And many seek some guidance by pursuing other ways
of spiritual advancement by invoking prayer and praise,
or lives in isolation to renounce the human-state
and dedicate themselves, instead, their souls to elevate.

Informed by Hindu-sages as perceived 'enlightened-souls'
on levels of awareness that can stand as spiritual-goals,
providing paths towards such goals to which all may aspire,
perhaps prescribed by scriptures or examples that inspire.

'God' is a label given to a 'Source' we do not know,
of 'Nature' or 'The Universe', from which all blessings flow.
It's beyond our comprehension that the Universe exists.
It's in this depth of mystery that need of faith persists.

We may beg for God's forgiveness for our many faults and flaws,
with assumption of God's loving-care, and universal-laws;
and since we have no knowledge of what is or isn't true,
in a search for explanation, we need to search for meaning too.

First Flight

I have an eighteenth-birthday gain,
to visit an aunt who lives in Spain.
Long sensed that flying is insane,
but now I'm trapped inside a plane.

Dear Lord, I pray to offer praise,
but have another point to raise.
Mankind was not designed to fly
and now I see the reason-why.

Please bring me gently back to Earth;
I'll never stray, for what that's worth.
I can get giddy standing up;
I'll stay at home and buy a pup.

Dear Lord, please let this plane not lurch;
I'll pray at temple, mosque or church.
I herewith renounce my sins;
this day my sinless-life begins.

First Flight

We 'cruise' at thirty-thousand-feet;
I'm rigid and glued to my seat.
For sex-impulse I'll seek a cure,
and entertain no thoughts-impure.

I missed the message, up that ladder
of painful pressure on my bladder.
Lord, bring me down, safe and secure;
send *earthbound* ordeals-to-endure.

To feel your Earth beneath my feet,
from flying let me fast-retreat;
 and keep me grounded through my days,
 and save my soul in other ways.

I feel this monster sway and jump,
my stomach knotted in a lump;
need message to rely upon,
we're up here with the wings still on.

I drool and dribble in descent
as rising panic won't relent.
Armrests squeezed with all my might,
eyes closed, heart clutched and knuckles white.
 *
I'm on firm ground to find Aunt May
warm in embrace, I hear her say,
'How was your flight, was all all-right?'
'No-sweat!' I shrug. 'It's just a flight.'

Focus

These days I'm often finding that my focus goes astray
and I'm floundering to follow my routines throughout the day.
I could be in the kitchen when my flow just seems to stop
and I'm wondering if I'm aiming for a mince pie or a mop.

Some moments might immerse the mind in temporary trance,
until connection *re*-occurs, my memory to enhance.
No doubt it's part of ageing, one more *in*sult to incur,
the blocking of awareness to a state of mental-blur.

I'm waiting at my wash basin; what am I doing there?
Did I come in to brush my teeth or just to comb my hair?
And why have I so lost the plot by memory-deprived
and able just to *wait* until awareness is revived?

I was never over*bur*dened by the brain-cells I received,
prefer they function when in need, reliably perceived,
without resorting to time-off to interrupt the flow
and implement a mental-pause to render progress slow.

I think I've found a way that could this vexing problem solve,
to which I must commit myself with credible resolve,
by consciously deflecting all diversions-of-the-mind,
denying any scope for such distractions to unwind,

for it's always such distractions that cause memory-lapse to form
and for focus to be *side*lined and so ceasing to inform;
but by distraction held at bay, first-focus keeps free space,
no interruption to its flow, and memory in place.

We must suppress those wanderings within our mental-range,
manipulate our mental-flow in ways that *we* arrange;
directing our awareness in any way we can,
so that our focus be maintained by practice and by plan.

All per*haps* a little daunting and less easy than it seems,
and, mentally, re*duc*ing flow as much as it redeems;
but protection of our focus surely serves to best effect
in permitting us to function and preserve our self-respect.

Gambler

For sure, this is my final spin
from rags to riches with one win.
I watch each card slot into place,
my hopes soon sunk without a trace.

But wait—what difference is one more?
Not knowing what Fate has in store.
That definitely *was* the last;
so crushed by how the cards were cast.

I've sat too long at this machine;
it's seeming miserable and mean.
And yet, a pay-out must be due;
so far, it's offered far too few.

By leaving now, how will I feel,
or watch another player steal
some treacherously rich reward,
fat with cash I can't afford?

So hard to bring myself to leave,
with much I'm anxious to retrieve
and pay-out pecking at my door,
my ache to ease, my faith restore.

To mounting pressure I'll submit,
with calling coins I can commit
in certainty of kind success
to foil much flirting with excess.

Oh, God, I have less than I thought,
intruders for my focus fought,
attention missing from my mind,
with care and caution far behind.

And now I find just five coins left,
my spirit broken and bereft,
my stomach-rumble long ignored;
could one more spin see all restored?

A First Touch of Reality (Gap-Year)

Hi, Mum, from icy-England, now
no sweat, but frost around my brow;
my gap-year's sure brought a change
with some adjustment to arrange.

I thought March brought the English-Spring,
flowers to bloom and birds to sing;
instead of rents to make me sob
with no real access to a job.

Please don't worry, I'll be fine,
but pray the sun may on me shine—
for, yesterday, the toilet froze
and ice was forming on my nose.

*

I lost my wallet on packed train
and then sustained an ankle-sprain.
I can be frugal, never rash;
don't send more money, keep your cash.

*

I lost my footing, took a fall,
but hardly hurt myself at all;
just skinned a knee and bruised an arm
and didn't suffer serious harm.
*

Had to buy some warmer-wear,
and walking now to pay no fare;
no heater in the room at night,
and, so far, not a job in sight.
*

Thanks for new money that you sent;
with prices high, it's quickly spent.
In truth, there's nothing left to spare
and items needing some repair.
*

Best cut my losses, change my flight,
head home defeated; you were right.
You've now sent more than you could spare;
I'll pay you back, of that I swear.
*

I'm now withdrawing words-of-woe,
so please withhold the 'told-you-so'.
This week brings welcome weather-change
and 'rescue' ready to arrange.
*

Ran into someone I once knew,
whose flatmate's leaving-time is due;
inviting me to fill that space—
and she's attractive, by God's-grace.

Ghost writer

At first, I didn't know I'd died,
despite prone body by my side.
I'd simply turned, somehow slid out,
and tried, in vain, to scream and shout.

I kept my mind from panic spared;
for dying I was ill-prepared,
for death's not due at twelve-years-old,
despite last winter's wicked cold.

I found that I was free to float
and felt inclined to leave a note
to state my wishes and my needs,
express remorse for all misdeeds,

and mourn lost time a trail-to-blaze,
secure success and steep in praise,
and leave a legacy to boast—
not relegation to a ghost.

I floated to my writing-space
with pens and notepads set in place;
to render all on record then,
but helpless to pick up a pen.

But then, I quickly came to find
by firmly focusing my mind;
I could implore the pen to flow,
controlled, across the page below.

And so, I came to then record
this story that seemed faintly flawed
and, as I wrote, some questions rose
to strongly on my mind impose.

Am I dreaming, can I wake
from such a nightmare, for my sake?
And, with that thought, I promptly woke,
still shaken by the spell that broke.

Homeless

My mother is an invalid, my father is a drunk,
It was apparent, at sixteen, how low my life had sunk
when some small slip would set him off into a drunken rage,
and I'd become his target by that God-forsaken stage.

I packed a few essentials in the middle of the night
and silently departed, mailing notes on mother's plight.
I had four-hundred dollars that I thought would see me through
as I caught a train to Sydney with an optimistic view.

The bustle-of-big-cities brought my first need to adjust,
but basic burger-breakfast had become a pressing 'must';
then searching out some local job for which I might apply,
'experienced' the road-block, however hard I'd try.

The 'Y.M.' had a 'full'-sign and a boarding-house seemed best,
but no vacancies existed and I badly needed rest.
I wandered round the city-streets, not knowing where to seek,
a weary walk with sinking heart and *all* hope rendered weak.

In fading light, I stumbled on a part of Martin Place
where homeless people gathered, and I settled for a space,
but for the coolness of the night, I was sorely ill-equipped,
so, sleep was scant, discomfort stamped the state to which I'd slipped.

From sitting-pose, to drowse and drift, I roused myself at dawn,
felt dirty and dishevelled and despairing and withdrawn,
found escalator-in-descent to train-station below,
there to relieve my bladder and to wash with water-flow.

Too late, I had a *sense* of stealthy movement from behind,
a sudden shock of pain and then a misty, muddled mind.
When someone helped me to my feet, my face felt stiff and swollen.
Instinctively, I quickly checked, to find my money stolen.

Back on the street, I saw a van dispensing scones-and-tea,
and queued to take advantage of such service, given free.
I found some cardboard, in a bin, on which to seal my fate
in printed-plea to passers-by that stressed my homeless-state.

Hopes

I hope you have a good night's sleep with re-assuring dreams,
and wake-and-rise tomorrow to a day when sunshine streams
in through your window, to give warmth in every way,
and provide you with a happy place, preparing for the day;

and may adventure bless you and good-fortune be your friend,
and any road-blocks be removed, and peaceful paths extend.
I'll always have you in my thoughts, and plead in every prayer,
may days protect and nourish you with tender, loving care.

We must accept we can't foresee all that the future holds
as we ad*apt* to each new stage, however life unfolds,
and always be supportive of the choices that we make,
and be at hand with ready help, however high the stake.

May aspiration reap reward, providing all you need,
permitting you to stay un*spoilt* in seeking to succeed;
enriching all around you with your giving, gracious style
as you lift us with your laughter and sustain us with your smile.

I'm imagining ahead, of course, projecting thought through time,
since human-paths have hurdles and some solid hills to climb.
I'm steering you past problems in maternal mental-drift,
for your safety and wellbeing form, for me, God's greatest gift.

You are my constant focus in all futures I can see;
I must repel possessiveness, prepare to set you free,
even though the thought of that can freeze my heart with fear
and never can occur without the shedding of a tear.

Why should the future be im*posed* upon the present day,
when all is seeming perfect and with no cause for dismay?
Why should my mind be dwelling on such distant days ahead;
why not enjoy the present, *free* from future paths-to-tread?

I hope you had a good night's sleep, with reassuring dreams,
to rise into this sun-soaked day, as searching as it seems.
I'll trust, along life's path ahead, my hopes will stay alive,
now focused on first day-at-school, now that you're turning five.

H.S.C.

I think I've tanked the H.S.C. with deepening despair,
previous tensions tease my mind, but nothing can compare.
I find the waiting wilting, but awareness may be worse;
computer-access to results a blessing or a curse?

One moment that may strike me down with such ferocious force,
with such depth-of-devastation, as disastrous as divorce;
from juicy-carrot-of-success along the road ahead
to desperation and decline to poverty instead.

I clowned around in classes and resisted being taught,
misplacing my priorities to be obsessed with sport;
embraced no midnight-swotting and refused to 'pay-my-dues',
to now be facing failure from which misery ensues.

I know reactions are in place, should shame assault my screen,
we'll all feign cool composure that can keep life calm and clean;
Dad's catch-cry of 'God-give-me-strength' and Mum's 'still-love-you' stare;
Dad only needs my company; Mum's mask brings guilt-to-bear.

Quite recently, it does so seem, demands were less severe,
sixteen-year-olds could exit school with nothing much to fear;
university was focused most on medicine or law,
but now we need some set-degree to scrub the office floor.

I'm in the execution-cell, past praying for reprieve,
and searching in my sorry brain for last, sad words to leave.
While schoolmates proudly punch the air, on pathways to success,
I'll be the much-scorned classroom-clown who only left a mess.

For fools like me, all doors will close and firmly shut me out,
for self-indulgent disregard of what 'real life's' about;
left painfully to scramble for some casual-job at best,
or plunged to depths of petty-crime while warding off arrest.

It's pointless to procrastinate, I'm sure results are known;
I only need to check the screen on which my fate is shown.
My finger floats above the key, I brace to be harassed.
It may be merely average but, My God! My God, I've passed!!

In Praise of Trees

I so seek comfort from the trees,
leaf-clusters bustling in the breeze;
strong trunks on which all can rely
with some seen stretching for the sky,

and might of Nature long-endured,
with ease that renders us assured
of something stable and secure,
somehow portraying life-more-pure,

providing wood to work or burn,
requiring nothing in return,
but be benign and cause no harm,
to bleak locations bring some charm;

inferred familiarity of friends,
immovable, immune from trends,
supplying shelter as required,
freely offered and acquired,

a source of sanctuary for all,
and sense-of-safety to install,
from extreme weather to protect,
with service worthy of respect;

providing homes for all the birds
and insect-life in hordes and herds;
and jungle-dwellers to sustain,
permitting apes life-to-retain.

Providing food that we consume,
our right to which we all assume
and never pause to thank the trees
while fondling fruit with juice to squeeze.

Absorb pollution from the air,
removing menace lurking there,
providing us with means to breathe
and essence of our lives bequeath.

Is Birthright Right?

We learn of cuts to foreign-aid,
with hopes of starving kids betrayed
as others follow Government-lead,
denying those in desperate need;

how easy to ignore the plight
of those remote and out-of-sight;
excuse at hand if so required,
conscience-pressure now expired.

Could we include, for concerned care,
impoverished people *everywhere*;
reach out to all those, far or near,
entrapped in suffering or in fear.

*

Is the effort such a task,
compassion just too much to ask,
and are there boundaries set in place
to limit love, confine embrace?

Or should we view the way ahead
in terms of world-wide-needs instead;
perhaps reject, with head and heart,
those lines to keep us all apart?

And all concede the luck involved
in births where lifestyles are resolved,
where some may live in pampered peace
with others screaming for release.

And should those favoured with best luck
stay blessed by life's sweet fruit to pluck,
without a backward glance at those
that fate or fortune never chose?

And should we therefore just ignore
the cries of those beyond our shore;
embrace the luck that birth bestows,
forbid compassion to impose,

stay free beneath our friendly skies,
which distant-birth so much denies,
as we relax, so safe and sure,
so well-provided and secure?

And should we just *assume* we're worth
unearned advantages of birth—
or seek out suffering and assist
and can't both concepts co-exist?

Just Kidding

She comes with that Sushmita-look,
and laughs a lot, and likes to cook
and do the housework every day,
and lift all lives in every way.

It takes no time before she speaks;
she masters English in two weeks,
and loves to talk and loves to write
and hogs the laptop, day and night,

and sees at once that life's a game,
and sets her sights on wealth and fame;
exploits the power of the pen,
with millions made before she's ten,

all gifted to her mum and dad
to keep them happy, never sad;
safe in their mansion by the sea,
completely work-and-worry-free.

That's how it was in Arjun's dream,
but things aren't always what they seem;
now prompting thoughts to re-arrange,
confronting one more nappy-change.

Location Rules

I don't possess a bicycle, a motorbike or car.
Instead, I'm now located where nothing is too far,
requiring five-minutes' walk to services-and-shops,
close to a railway-station, and also bus-route-stops.

I don't possess a mobile phone, not presently 'online'.
No access to the internet, but postal-mail is fine.
Don't have a com*pute*r, social-media declined,
no digital-devices and no urges so inclined.

I'm satisfied to walk around in comfort and in peace,
without demands of contact that never seem to cease.
Instead, enjoy the sunshine and flow-of-life around,
and the solid reassurance of gravity-and-ground,

and sand-and-sea, and parkland also very near,
and necessary services so well-provided here.
I used to wander wide-and-far, but now refuse to roam,
since all enjoyed in foreign-parts can be enjoyed at home.

I never eat at restaurants, or *buy* coffee outside,
as it's so much cheaper to be *home* and self-provide,
and keep control of quantity, and quality as well,
and easier to keep contained unwanted waistline-swell.

I'm sure I don't deny myself in any way or form,
adhering to a simple life, refusing to conform;
socialising as I choose, succumbing to no urge
to create some constant-contact into which I then submerge.

I use my local library, and also local club,
and read a daily newspaper, not tempted to the pub,
engage in television-sport, connect by landline-phone,
remain relaxed and occupied, content to live alone.

Of course, we must depend upon our functioning and health,
aspects that must far exceed perceived 'success' or wealth;
and human bond-and-friendship is a treasured aspect too.
I'm happy as a head-of-hair, approaching eighty-two.

Luck?

So grateful for all help received and useful lessons learned,
for all rewards for effort and for everything I've earned;
my family and friends from whom I always draw such strength,
and for whose health-and-happiness I'd go to any length.

For parents who prepared me for the pressures life imposed,
prevented me from straying, or to danger be exposed;
protected me in many ways to keep me safe and well,
provided me with all my needs, warm home in which to dwell,

appreciating all the luck that offers life a lift,
including in appearance, so grateful for that gift;
detached from disadvantages or burdens-to-be-borne,
subjected to no bigotry or prejudicial scorn,

was so glad for national-*service* and that disciplining-time;
that I've never suffered violence or been victim of a crime.
I've mostly loved the life I've lived in happiness-and-health;
I'm only slightly envious of those born into wealth.

The occurrence of a plane-crash and the loss of several lives,
with the shock of stricken children and the
widowhood-of-wives;
so stained my soul with tragedy and suffering sustained,
but grateful-still my friends were safe and friendships were retained,

so grateful that my flights were smooth and turbulence subdued,
with safety never *compromised* as flying-time accrued,
no incident to cause concern, on confidence impact,
and gratitude would grow with each return-to-earth-intact.

I do reflect and wonder at all suffering in the world,
so many lives afflicted as if *into* hell-flames hurled;
so many victims, of vile violence or of need,
so many desperate people and so many mouths to feed.

How much is really gratitude, how much reflects relief,
avoiding being victims of such unforgiving grief?
I question my good fortune and the blessed life I live,
with gratitude to offer *help* and, most of all, to *give*.

My Message

To make this Christmas-message right,
I'm striving hard with all my might
while disregarding mental strain
and protest from my ageing brain.

Some sentiments I *must* convey
to help your spirit *soar* all day;
to do you justice, as I must
to *all* I most respect and trust.

To best express my high esteem
in ways directed by a dream
that indicate the light you are;
a guide to others, *near* and far.
*

I've persevered with the need
to send a poem, ripe to read
that seeks to brighten *any* mood
with words to leave you feeling good.

One Way

Though blessed too much to understand,
by birth, into this lucky land,
where all are equal under law,
no human-state is free from flaw.

We crave fine features, frame and form,
all aspects that Fate may deform,
inflicting flaws in many ways,
deflate life's flow from early days.

No 'image' should be met by scorn,
but to appearance most seem drawn;
peer-acceptance plays prime part,
rejection may such pain impart.

May help to be astute or smart,
deflecting arrows-to-the-heart,
but most are helpless to resist,
and isolation may persist.

So how hold hope to face each day
and keep rejection held at bay?
It needs capacities to cope,
with ways to cultivate that hope.
*

It starts with attitude-of-mind,
to sideline doubt and seek to find
activities that should support
involvement—such as any sport.

Perhaps you're short or overweight,
can't interact or can't relate,
baulked by impediment of speech,
subdued by standards you can't reach,

or tainted teeth or pock-marked skin,
face too fat or arms too thin,
or stuttering that makes you shy,
or slow to grasp or to comply.

Birth-base imbalance tends to bring
for some, such lonely songs to sing.
One way by which defy distress—
set goals and focus on success.

Perceptions

In need of some sound meaning, young and old aspire to seek,
to pause, prepared to listen to the way that spirits speak,
and in some mystic-moments seem to stumble on some truth
grasped with *caut*ion by the ageing or with eagerness by youth.

Such moments seem to be quite rare, not readily enhanced,
nor leading to some lasting-light by which to be *entranced*.
For most, the core-persuasion of a 'message-from-above'
sits in sensing a Creator who exudes engulfing love.

Religions *produ*ce different names for that 'Creative-Source',
sometimes involving 'messengers' with urgings to enforce,
that *can* cause separation and hostility to rise,
with risk of being violent in pretence of being wise.

It takes a putrid path-to-plod to follow such a 'god',
bowing to the force-of-fear and ruled by iron-rod.
No normal person seeks a 'god' intent on spreading hate;
each strives to find the source-of-love to which they may relate.

But 'God' is just a name we give, in prayers we wish to send,
a label for 'Creative-Source' that none can comprehend;
the Source that causes all-that-is and all that we perceive,
a source from which we all can seek best blessings to receive.

Our universe accelerates, expanding into space
with galaxies, in *billions*, contained in its embrace;
each galaxy with *billions* of planets and of stars,
all infinitely more complex than manmade motorcars.

And on *this* tiny planet, as it hurtles on through space,
a myriad of creatures live, besides the human-race;
animals and insects and lifeforms of the seas,
birds-that-fly, and flowers, and thriving plants and trees.

And all is fully functioning, with order that astounds,
with cycles that are followed and set-patterns so profound.
For those who seek 'Creative-Source', no trace is ever found;
no evidence that 'God' exists—except for all-around.

Life In Spirit (Perhaps)

When our brains no longer function and our bodies are deceased,
when human-form is left behind and spirit is released,
does there remain some sense of 'self', identity-retained?
Without our body-parts in play, can process be explained?

Deprived of physicality, how do we then adjust?
When nothing known remains intact, new mindset is a must,
somehow perceiving all that's gone and what has come to be;
are we falling off a mountain or, more, climbing up a tree?

Perhaps commence by listing many aspects left behind,
before we can consider if the change is cruel or kind.
Much must depend on circumstance or sufferings or strife,
so, need assume 'normality', assessing human-life.

So many aspects now deleted by discarded human-form
to now proceed in spirit and profoundly different 'norm'.
No struggle now to just survive, with brutal bills to pay,
or pressing needs to which attend, address without delay.

No need to wash the dishes, nor taking out the trash,
or tending to a nosebleed or to little-Roland's rash,
or rushing to be ready, delayed by unmade-bed,
or worried to be late for work, or by demands ahead.

No struggle with a toenail clip, to shower or to shave,
no need for brushing of the teeth, or make the hair behave,
no useless searching for clean socks, deciding how to dress,
no fretting over feature-flaws or defects that depress.

No fear of dreaded ailment or of our pending fate,
or sufferings of those we love, to whom we most relate;
no detrimental ageing or distress from any cause,
no heartbreaks or disasters, and no violence or wars.

Our human-journey may be blessed by well-being and peace,
but, for most, with times of torment from which to beg release;
so overall will spirit-life mean better way-to-be,
all automatically attached while feeling fully free?

Awareness, our new way-of-life, unruled by day or night,
when everything will be repaired and all regrets made right,
and everything made possible by simplest wish or prayer,
requiring just our quiet need to place us anywhere.

Respect

The milk-money collected and his classmates' smirks suppressed,
the lonely boy stands at the front, pain by-his-eyes expressed,
his task to count the coins aloud, his face so flushed in shame;
he can't subdue his stutter and has no escape to claim.

He's 'teacher's warning' to the class, of power that he wields,
authority embedded by a fear that this yields;
the victim just a useful tool to keep a class subdued
that order may remain intact by smothered attitude.

The boy must flee the classroom when the final period ends,
engulfed in some consuming cloud as torture then extends.
Home-bound, entrapped by taunts, that pile the pressure on his head,
to seek seclusion in his room, with bitter tears shed.

The stutter dominates his teens; his dreams are rarely spared;
self-confidence remains subdued, performance much impaired.
He fails all tests imposed by schools with no success to show,
then wrestles job-rejections as his aggravations grow.

*

His father left when he was small and he's an only child.
He has no friends, but to that fact he's sadly reconciled,
increasingly reclusive as he rarely ventures out,
his tendency to alcohol offset by money-drought.

His mother is a cleaner who seems prematurely-aged,
herself withdrawn and, with her son, by circumstances, caged,
so, there's basic-interaction, but they neither smile nor sob.
Unnoticed, now he turns eighteen; still hasn't had a job.

He's not known how to cause a change or anything that can,
until, one day, he's stunned to find his mother's met a man,
but he can't avoid the issue when the knock comes to his door.
He just wants a hole to open; to be swallowed by the floor.

He finds a man of average looks and 'lived-in' middle-age,
his glasses and his greying hair complete the profile-page.
'I'm Ian, here to date your mum, but want to check with you.
May I come in, just briefly, so that *you* can check *me* too!

'I fully understand your plight; I stuttered all through school.'
A calmness seems to fill the room and everything seems cool.
'I'd love to visit you each day and coach to best effect.
I *can* prescribe a 'magic-pill—my unrestrained respect.'

The Pimple

Young Tony's late for school today,
tricks his hair, no trace of grey;
he spots a strand that's gone astray,
decides it's cuter left that way.

Fifteen-years-old and free to roam,
secure still with stable home,
can concentrate, without real cause,
on fretting over facial flaws.

A single pimple, now perceived,
produces panic, unrelieved,
with devastation quite complete,
romantic-hopes in full retreat.

And yet his face is finely formed,
teeth intact and eyes informed,
narrow nose and jutting jaw;
a face that artists ache to draw.

Protruding pimple still persists
in trapped-attention that insists
on plunging Tony into doubt
and more delay in going out.

But, culprit covered up with cream,
brain set to stifle any scream,
he circumvents the TV-news
that strains all senses to abuse.

By fierce fire, or by flood,
or battlefields so drenched in blood.
Paramedics cruise his street
for bruised or broken bones to treat.

But all seems silent, still and calm,
exuding sadness, not alarm,
with doorway-dwellers well apart—
alone to deal with daytime-start.

*

He knows the bundled forms are live
with daunting days through which to strive,
but *his* space, also, is preserved
and by detachment better served.

A blaring ambulance blasts by
and startled birds stretch for the sky,
but people-pain is held at bay,

denied impact on Tony's day.

Returning home, his mind stays closed,
no suffering to be imposed.
His door can block out people-plights,
with sleep protected through the nights.
*

But apprehension penetrates,
aroused uneasiness awaits
the mirror's call, expanding dread,
disaster, should the pimple spread.

The Power

My memory spans eighty years
through times of anguish and of fears,
initially by bully-boy
immersed in mission to destroy.

Target and taunt some smaller kids,
entrapping us beneath bin-lids
to harass and humiliate,
as panic-pitch would escalate.

And next, in later years at school,
where gang style-groups are acting 'cool'
to stake their claim to 'power-pack',
provoking victims-to-attack.

Also, some teacher, insecure;
of his authority unsure,
feels the need of order to assert
by potent put-downs to insert.

And national-service intervenes,
sadistic drilling that demeans,
self-worth expunged without a trace
by obscene screaming in the face.

And on it goes, all now recalled,
with reconstruction since installed,
self-respect now on display
and introspection now in play.

*

Now on so much I must reflect
to stabilise such self-respect.
Was it enough just to survive,
subdue the storm and stay alive?

I dwell on shortcomings and flaws,
impose my own insights and laws;
now that the focus is on *me*,
for from myself I may not flee.

Set goodness as my only goal,
a need-now-felt to free my soul,
submit to love, by which to live;
engage the power—to forgive.

Politics

Finances are in focus when elections come around,
politicians make their pitches and their promises abound;
as parties slot their chants in place to find a song to sing,
and if the song seems out-of-tune, they find some mud to fling.

They intercept us on the street to hone in on our votes,
adjusting spiel to our response, whatever that denotes;
from plenty prepared answers that anticipate our groans,
invade the mailbox with their pleas and infiltrate our phones.

Each side has key statistics, well selected for support,
at which opponents sneer, with disdain or rude retort;
with tax-and-targets at the core, which points persuade the most
to steer the economic-ship toward a calmer coast?

While other issues are produced, they rarely dominate,
and handling-the-economy seems always to dictate,
as propaganda swamps us all and only facts are changed,
and claims become outrageous with history rearranged.

Those favoured by inheritance, by lottery of birth,
can live a life of luxury and watch the 'war' with mirth;
no need to struggle or compete, no need to 'make a case',
encouraged by a *tax*-haven both parties keep in place.

Each party has a point-to-prove in typical debates;
boosting of big-business-wealth to which the 'Right' relates,
or 'fairer' distribution, to which the 'Left' aspires,
as platitudes spew out each day, no cliché ever tires.

The 'Left' wants tax-cuts that could help the struggling 'working-class',
including those-who-can't-find-work in one expanding mass.
The 'Right' protects, with tender care, the rich 'top-end-of-town',
so 'worker-ants' can then collect some crumbs that trickle down.

So, the parties are divided as they've always been before,
with revenue-control the prize in frenzied tug-of-war,
and when it comes to voting, we can choose what fits our need—
the politics-of-envy or the politics-of-greed.

Pressing On

I never *planned* a marathon
as years spun by to eighty-one.
I ponder on the life I've led
and contemplate a path ahead.

Indulge myself to dwell upon
sweet youth and early years long gone.
With hindsight from this advanced stage,
what blessings could I *have* engaged?

To what aspire or to strive,
how best to keep my dreams alive;
how to decide and how to start,
with whom to join and when to part;

when to accept and when resist,
when to concede and when persist,
when to review and when to leave,
how to forgive, and how to grieve;

and with life-knowledge at my hand,
could I just grasp and understand
all problems posed, how to proceed,
with certainty I would succeed?

But with such knowledge ready-formed,
the benefit of being informed,
all learning aspects would be lost,
avoiding growth at heavy cost,

for steps of learning form a way
to offer meaning to each day,
providing purpose to press on
that need not end at eighty-one,

with rise and fall, and love and loss,
with hills to climb and streams to cross,
and time stretched out with no clear sign
of distance to the finish-line.

Putting It Politely

The memories of long-lost youth can cast a dream-locked spell.
The body bends or blunders; but the brain seems bound to dwell.
When I left school, in England, national-service was in play,
Two years enslaved, to shape us up the military-way.

All able-bodied, late-teen boys the Army ached to greet,
with no escape for those deemed 'straight', not blessed with two flat feet.
It was a test in many ways, with freedom so betrayed,
and all entrapped in poverty, with 'homeless' better-paid.

A one-stripe-moron's paradise of victims-on-parade,
obscenities-on-steroids, abuse a tool-of-trade.
Bare barrack-rooms for 'bullying' boots to acid-tongue attacks,
and distance-runs in whiplash-winds, with over-loaded packs.

Woken up in freezing nights to form-in-lines outside,
and left to shake and shiver, for lance-corporals to deride.
I'd think of my deluded mum and codes by which she'd live,
where even modest swear-words were not easy to forgive.

Mum, this is the only letter that we are allowed to write,
if I can first free-up my hands, preventing frost to bite.
Just returning from the cookhouse when we pass the drilling-square,
where an intervening sergeant seemed to have some time to spare.

*

'Stand still, you (toilet-house),' bawled he.
'You're shy to salute that (censored) officer, I see?'
'But, Sarge, he is so far away that I was unaware.'
'You need a (censored) eye-test and to get yourself a pair.'

'Your purpose is saluting every officer, bar none.'
'Now (censored) march ahead, salute each lamp-post—*every* one.'
I followed his instructions; didn't dare to glance behind,
until past the final lamp-post, no trace of him to find.

'You'll notice, Mum, through brackets, that I may have made some change.
Vocabularies are, here, based on body-parts and range.
Male-parts and their engagements seem to penetrate all speech.
Some editing enables me to practise what *you* preach.'

'I don't want to alarm you and I wouldn't want to whinge,
but I contemplate conscription with a tendency to cringe.
This letter will be censored, so I can't describe the food.
Please ignore the aspects mentioned and view everything as good.'

*

Rain

I understand the anguish caused by any prolonged drought,
but from personal perspective and my need to walk about,
I'm opposed to wet conditions and I've never relished rain,
wish less swelled-to-pavement pools and more went down the drain.

I hate to feel so trapped indoors, impatient to go out,
with apprehension to be drenched, my daily-plans to flout.
Age has brought me caution, with my comfort to protect,
but also, late aloneness, too much time in which reflect.

The mind, without distraction, finds a tendency to brood
and dwell on past-life's darker-days more often than it should.
That needs to be avoided by engagement with each day,
embracing aspects we enjoy, that work to light the way.

To walk around in comfort tends to keep the mind at peace,
with some restful sense of freedom, of relief and of release,
by parts of every passing day rewardingly so-spent,
mobility in any form embraced to best extent.

Rain renders us discomfort and dampens spirits too.
From pensioner-perspective then, the positives are few.
It causes cancellation of horse-race-fixtures due,
and disrupts the TV-cricket that we've settled down to view.

Weather-forecasts can be wrong and confidence be folly.
Some sudden change can catch you out and left without a brolly.
Protective doorways won't present, shop-awnings not at hand,
shelter at some distance, and no mercy-on-demand.

Must surrender to a soaking, with wet-and-clinging clothes,
confront that struggle-to-restore that everybody loathes.
Potential then for coughs and colds with sniffs and sneezes rife
with all the rude intrusion on a peaceful daily life.

Good weather is so crucial to our overall content,
and to much interruption I'm not ready to consent.
While whinging will not help a lot, I make my protest known.
Not blaming politicians, but I'm trapped inside to moan.

I do accept we need some rain, a point that must be stressed.
It could present a cause for my complaint to be suppressed.
I can't propose all rain should cease, with not a drop in sight,
I'll only ask, by natural law, it only rains at night.

Seeking the Way

Early in the eighties, today's technology unborn,
a letter, full of anguish, left me frozen and forlorn.
I'd spent some time in England, bonding family and friends,
prodding aspects upon which resettlement depends.

Australia had served me well, with much to offer still;
firm friendships well-established there, with happy hopes to fill;
and now a close-friend's brother writes with urgency released,
that close-friend lost in India, communication long since ceased.

I had experience of India and knew I had to go
to start a search at last-used bank with hope some clues may flow.
I had no work-commitments, with my pockets starved of cash,
and any ready options seemed too reckless and too rash.

I could scrape *some* notes together for due train-fares, leaving few
to test a roulette-system in casino I well knew;
all ending at the Tube-station, distraught, at Leicester-Square,
desolate, defeated and reduced to desperate prayer.

I shuffled to a public phone to sadly contact 'home'.
Had I *believed* that gambling could release me, free to roam?
On the phone-shelf sat a wallet to deflect my mental-ramble,
the contents revealed forty pounds. The owner's name was *Gamble!*

I had strong spiritual-beliefs and pleadingly had prayed,
and was in awe at clarity and speed of signs displayed.
I left the station, soon to find a beckoning betting-shop.
For forty pounds, a winning-double should permit me then to stop.

Selections simply based upon the return that I'd need,
for rescue-mission in my mind, wherever that may lead.
I thought the signs had shown me that success was guaranteed,
that higher-help had intervened; from failure I'd been freed.

The first race brought correction when my horse refused to start;
left stranded at the barrier to take no further part.
A violent storm erupted, complete with clouds of dust,
cracks opened in the ceiling; I was through the exit thrust.

I cleaned myself as best I could to set off homeward-bound,
with plenty time to contemplate my misuse of funds-found.
Back home, I posted wallet-docs, with promise to repay
before I left for India, with *loans* to pave my way.

Sleep

If dwelling on world-woes would make us weep,
we may always seek escape to soothing sleep,
while wishing to redeem, not to depress,
from which to wake refreshed, free from distress,

if not too high a help for which to ask,
when finding sleep itself may prove a task,
with restlessness, persistent toss-and-turn,
and time-in-bed that seems like time-to-burn.

But from sound-sleep, the benefits derived
are sadly missed when we are sleep-deprived
and intrusions on our sleep cause us to curse,
at sounds perhaps, with bladders always worse.

Duration of our sleep seems much discussed,
and many see eight-hours as a 'must'.
Margaret Thatcher insisted *that* the need was only four,
perhaps with aspirations to embed it in the law.

Perhaps she had a reason for her strangle-hold on sleep;
she had to stop the unions, and all wars, and bracket-creep,
and so she settled for less sleep, since four was all required,
with some brave soul to wake her once four hours had expired.

Another bedtime-issue is uncertainty of dreams
imposed upon our nightly-sleep, like movies so it seems,
and sometimes scary nightmares when our sleep produces plight,
tormented by our terror, and with no escape in sight.

But torment can take other forms, like partners who snore,
until, distraught and desperate, we can't take it anymore.
Even *subdued* snores incite, however faint or humble,
a slightly softer form-of-hell than endless earthquake-rumble,

catastrophe to come between a husband and his wife;
but still *sleep's* a central aspect in our 'quality-of-life',
so that our nights can be a pleasure *or* a plight,
with *any* day depending on how well we slept last night.

The Blessing

First time I'd idly drifted down
to this flea-market part of town;
small shops, in narrow, dusty streets,
that stocked old books and faded sheets

and furniture, all second-hand
and obscure objects, on demand.
Aimed to arrive at opening-time
when cocks would crow and clocks would chime

and shops would open with no fuss,
nor chat, nor topics to discuss,
before some bustle might emerge
and bargains bring a buying-surge.

An ancient man, from a tiny shop,
emerged ahead with pail and mop,
but, as I watched, his body bent,
and knees betrayed his best intent.

Still silent, to the ground he fell,
unmoving, seeming in a spell.
Location-trapped, with no retreat,
I helped him to regain his feet,

and eased him back inside his shop,
there on some cheap, chipped chair to flop;
and at the rear found a tap,
cold water woke him like a slap.

Awareness sparked within his eyes,
no trace of tension or surprise,
face oriental, shrivelled skin
and, when he spoke, the voice was thin,

but clear, and *accent*-less it seemed,
somehow remote as if I dreamed.
'Child, your help is well-received,
leaves me recovered and relieved.

Your kindness must now be repaid
by blessing that will never fade.
Long life I can bestow to you,
with sweet success in all you do.

Not able to myself accord,
reserved for others as reward,
the fruits of which may be assessed
when looking back on life-well-blessed.

Of course, back then, I *was* a child
still aimless, and a little wild,
without ambition or set goal,
unformed for *any* future role.

But now I'm eighty-and-a-day,
still with strong health in every way.
I won't say that I've known no strife,
but *have* felt blessed throughout my life.

The Brother

At the service, all *tri*butes flowed to you,
and some were flawed, but also most were true;
still, some of it you'd surely view with scorn,
with widened eyes, dismissive grin, well-worn.

You still remain an 'angel' to Aunt-Sue,
the role produced when pocket-money due.
What neighbour's urgent *need* did you once meet,
now to earn you 'heartbeat-of-the-street'?

Protected now from consequence of plots
like stink-bomb-greetings served through letter-slots,
that favoured-fad when you were eight years old,
a trial-time, when truth was rarely told.

Some schoolmate stood in order to extend
a eulogy to you, his now-lost friend;
how, for your mates, you'd take on any fight,
regardless of what was or wasn't right.

With loyalties so firmly formed and fixed,
I sometimes found myself with feelings mixed;
for you it meant the boon of many friends,
with personal-worth which, from that, best-extends.

Though, in age, I was two years ahead,
it seemed to be a lesser-life I led,
and while I slogged through grades at school,
your easy triumphs made me feel a fool.

The ease with which your star would shine
so brightly, when compared to mine.
I seemed too ready to resent,
for which now needing to repent.

And now I couldn't even speak;
all words within my head seemed weak.
You were kid-brother, pain and pest,
who always left me second-best.

No way did you deserve to die
by drunken-driver-blasting-by.
Too late to reach for words, now that you've left,
now leaving me, alone and lost ... b*ereft*.

The Decline

Don't care to climb up mountains, though I'm happy that they're there.
Don't ache to leap from aeroplanes, fall freely through the air.
Don't hope to hunt wild animals, appalled that they are killed.
Don't seek to swim the Channel as the concept leaves me chilled.

Could admire those who do so, but no longer see the point.
I can't descend to 'doing drugs', or even roll a joint.
Still happy to enjoy a drink, but now know when to stop,
while smoking offers cancer and a habit hard to drop.

Such things have teased and tested me along my lengthy life.
I've struggled not to side-track when temptations were so rife,
with so many caught in quicksand that I've striven to avoid,
while pressures of 'belonging' render people paranoid.

Inclined to be a 'local-boy' since age imposed it's hold,
now fussed by trivial issues such as coffee coming cold,
and I'm easily overwhelmed by such suffering everywhere;
in places where I spent some time without concern or care.

I never go to pubs these days, and scarcely socialise;
a local walk and flight-of-stairs complete my exercise.
I rarely sit in restaurants; eat sandwiches at home,
and local shops meet all my needs; no reason now to roam.

Reading has a part to play, as favourite friends do too.
I'm not above a modest bet (with winners overdue).
Television offers sport, to which I'm still so prone,
and I could produce a poem if I'm spending time alone.

Seems need of some avoidance as we keep the 'Beast' at bay,
in our process of adapting to all new demands in play,
but willing helpers often come, so most of us can cope,
and make adjustments, with that help, accepting smaller scope.

As friends must fall before the Beast, our strength may so deplete,
and how much damage will be done; how much left incomplete?
And how much loss can we absorb; how well can we adjust,
how much engage with changing times; maintain our hope and trust?

We can delay, but not defy, that final change to come,
and so, acceptance must be part, prepared we must become,
with access to a comfort-zone that 'passing' be quite calm,
and 'passing' means more moving-on, devoid of all alarm.

The Dilemma

I'm wondering what worries most on human-paths ahead;
the way seems blocked by obstacles no matter where we tread.
We see ourselves as each a 'self' with body, brain and face,
but also, as belonging to a collective human-race.

With instinctive apprehension that the human-race survive,
that Earth-and sun are stable, and people stay alive,
and Nature can construct a world where order can sustain,
and somehow patch the problems, that a future may remain,

and possibly preserve the peace, and planet, for us all,
and weave a way that will permit calm order to befall,
where caring and compassion can combine to fill the space,
and nations, if they *can't* combine, at least can stay in place,

respect each other's cultures for *full* peace to persist,
and by such code conduct themselves to calmly co-exist.
Confrontation is a cancer that contaminates all hope
with despair and desperation, and much grief with which to cope.

It's not that problems are obscure or don't affect us all,
and our attitudes determine if we stand erect or fall.
It seems we all need to accept all cultures with respect,
and improvise, and compromise as means to self-protect.

Including with our effort in addressing climate change
before due intervention becomes *too* late to arrange;
before all ice-shelves melt away and seas-and-oceans swell,
and swallow lands and districts in which many used to dwell,

and wipe out farms and fertile fields and food-supplies for all,
and impact upon production and reduce it to a crawl.
It's only will and willingness that serve the human-cause,
and should not be obstructed or ever put 'on-pause',

but only human-factors, as neglect or bad-intent,
can cause such devastation, so destructive in extent,
as we disrespect the planet by our reckless lack-of-care,
and still behave in ways to leave our world the worse-for-wear.

The Journey

We start with immature ways to measure human-worth,
defined by features of the face or growth of a girth.
Appearance the focal-point, obscuring so much more
that swims below the surface or a bit beyond the shore.

Like human-ants, we scurry round, intent to fill the day,
perhaps weighed down by problems or frustrated by delay,
or paralysed by burdens, either real or self-perceived,
or troubled by anxieties that never seem relieved.

We need to keep some time aside to search within ourselves.
A library has many books displayed on many shelves.
In taking time to study shelves we sometimes can connect
with books that can reward us in some ways we don't expect.

In delving deep inside ourselves, who knows what we may find,
or what encounters we may have beyond the brain or mind.
Could meditation dive so deep that we become aware
of the basis of our being with perceptions then stripped bare?

In India, belief is strong; we choose a birth to best belong,
deciding from a spirit-view, some move to sorrow or to song;
that previous paths prepare the way for karma to dictate
the circumstances of our birth and factors of our fate.

The human-path provides a means by which we all can grow,
in reaching past self-service, so to let compassion flow,
to feel the pain of others and of all in dire need,
direct our thoughts to those-at-risk and starving kids to feed.

If we see ourselves as separate, and so basically alone,
we may be missing many signs and ways we might have grown
and deplete best aspirations to a pre-determined goal
as spiritual-extensions of a Universal Soul.

If human-journeys point us at a wider spiritual plan,
awareness would prepare us all to serve as best we can.
If we are all connected as such aspects of that Soul,
then we should direct our journeys in pursuit of being whole.

The Prayer

How can I help you, son of mine;
implore in prayer, invoke some sign?
What can I do, what can I say
to drive persistent pain away?

Dear God, I've never prayed before;
my little boy, so sick, so sore.
Why should he suffer such a fate
so innocent at only eight?

Why is that driver not in jail,
for negligence, not brakes-that-fail?
He drove too fast, without due care,
with wandering mind too unaware.

Am I required to explain
all flaws permitted to remain,
and why I've never been to church
submerged in spiritual search?

So much of our religions seem so hard to understand;
we don't know why we're here and no answers are to hand.
Religious-text *describes* Divinity in human-form,
but Christianity commenced as calm-before-a-storm,

and a son so cruelly slaughtered in redemption of our sins;
if we also suffer torment, it *seems* that no-one wins;
my child is simply cast aside, a rag-doll or a toy;
I beseech you and I beg you, please repair my broken boy.

So much in sedation, so much surgery and stress,
so much anguish to erode us, so much anger to suppress;
such self-pity to engulf us, such a struggle to find peace,
so much sorrow to surround us, so much pressure to release.

All bringing us to blindly pray,
and stumble on in bleak dismay.
'Please spare my son and set him free
from *all* his pain, and punish *me*.'

'… should come … emergency … relapsed …';
some wall, within my soul, collapsed.
The voice vibrated in my ear.
'What?' pitched in panic, forged in fear.

'Emergency, has been declared …'
Beyond those words all else is blurred;
words that prodded, dipped in dread,
the dynamite within my head.

'Doctor coming, take a seat,'
No reassurance, no retreat.
'So sorry, but it's looking grim;
revival-prospects seeming slim;

his heart was still for far too long;
we've raised a pulse, but still not strong;
of consciousness, he shows no sign;
perhaps to loss we should resign.'

'Dear God, that isn't what I meant;
my plea was that his pain relent,
not that we lose him from our lives,
but please take *me* so he survives.'

Can he now know how much it means to watch him playing there?
For *I* know not how *I* survived that terrifying scare.
I've searched his gentle, caring eyes for clues that might emerge,
absorbed his boundless joy in play, embraced his every urge.

*

'What is it you remember of the time you were asleep?
Is everything forgotten as in dreams since buried deep?
Something must have happened to take your pain away
and make you so much better, as you seem to be today.'

He stares at me in some surprise, distracted from his game.
'Of course, Daddy, the pain has gone, and nothing is the same,
and I was happy where I was, but angels heard your prayer,
and told me that I could return into your loving care.'

The Search

Regardless of the paths we take
or any marks we aim to make,
life's not a contest or a race
and ageing-process stays in place.

There is a limit and an end
that human-journeys can't transcend
unless solution can be found
in some awareness, more profound,

that has no end and knew no start,
with human-pathways just a part
of longer journeys that involve
some essence striving to evolve.

Are we so *chained* to human-life,
to struggle with its stress and strife,
with inclination to ignore
an outcome just to *be* no more?

The body and the brain betray
our yearning for a better way;
from suffering provide release
while leaving us with love and peace.

Beyond this body and this brain,
we *sense* some essence free from pain.
In spirit-search should we engage
to seek the secrets of the sage?

Are we extensions of a soul,
that seeks to guide, but not control,
the human path we undertake,
somehow submerged, as in a lake?

Is it a lake we need to seek
and there implore our soul to speak,
intent to plumb a depth beyond
some surface-ripples on a pond?

The Separation

We press ahead with speed set low,
Conditions keep our progress slow.
A snaking road of curves and bends,
a dreamlike state that never ends.

This rusted car, in rough repair,
I need now drive with *ex*treme care.
We've come so far along this track,
there seems no way of turning back.

And with smooth surface in decline,
to which obstructions now combine,
should I approach with fear and dread
those pitfalls on the road ahead?

Or just surrender up my doubt
and keep my focus all about
strange sense of destination-changed,
as yet unknown, but pre-arranged.

*

There's a last despairing rattle as we shudder to a halt,
and a final anguished whimper like a yielding to assault,
and I feel a touch of sorrow, but the lingering is brief,
with a sense of separation, somehow tempered with relief.

I've loved this car that seems the one that served me best,
but I can't recall the others and attachment seems a test,
as some scattered shards of memory seem to slice into this mind
as I float out of the window, and I leave this car behind.

The Weekend

I've closed my eyes and searched my mind for worthy words to write,
without finding some solution, inspiration not in sight.
I've been around for fifty-years and never struck-it-rich,
now worrying that winter brings an irritating itch.

I tell myself I can't complain, it's wiser not to whinge,
but winds still make me shiver, crying-babies make me cringe,
I have no head for heights it seems, air-travel makes me sick;
I'm overcome by vertigo while standing on a brick.

I'm appalled by price-of-petrol, and that options seem so few,
or by premature waking with a wild dash for the 'loo',
or newspapers that trade upon disaster and abuse,
or political 'solutions' that seem never any use.

My painter-friend is paranoid, her paintings haven't sold,
and other people round me are succumbing to the cold.
It was a wearing week at work, with 'sickies' causing strife,
my best suggestions countered by advice to get-a-life,
by one obnoxious boss with whom it's always hard to live

because of rude remarks he makes, not easy to forgive.
I never seem to move ahead and always seem in debt,
a target for emerging clouds intent to make me wet.

So many are complaining at the pressures of a job,
and streets are sometimes cluttered by some cause-embracing mob.
Undue concerns lurk in each day, with readiness to pounce,
to pluck me up and drop me, just to see how high I bounce.

It's Saturday, the sun is high, the 'footy's' underway,
with mates around and beers-to-hand, the order of the day
in this blessed-and-lucky country, surrounded by blue sea;
there's not a place throughout the world that I would rather be.
*

Thought Control

In life-review, now fair to take,
back then, what changes would I make?
To dwell on that brings into play
so much regret and much dismay.

In watching other lives unfold,
despair seems   part of growing old.
Where am *I* going, what's my plan
now that *I'm* that 'older-man'?

It seems, perhaps a platitude,
but so much rests on attitude,
dependent on the way we *think*,
that moves our mood to soar or sink.

I need, perhaps, to train my mind
to set sad aspects far behind
and focus on what fosters hope;
not merely seeking how to cope,

and to that principle be bound,
if mental-faculties stay sound;
whatever setbacks lie ahead,
I *can* affect what's in my head,

never dwell on depressed thought,
remain in happy-pastures sought
and strive to stay always alert;
like trains, thoughts easy to divert,

and be prepared to store good thoughts,
achievements or success in sports,
or family-times or fun with friends,
all aspects from which love extends.

So set foundations, then to build
a 'mental-home' that's always filled
with happiness-and-love alone,
all trace of sadness to atone.

Assisted Voluntary-Euthanasia

I watched my father die today, with infinite relief,
to find myself then floundering in unforgiving grief.
His cancer had been well advanced, and 'Parkinson's' as well,
so many years he'd suffered an excruciating hell.

He didn't fully want to go, loved family and friends,
but believed that body-only dies, from which the soul ascends,
clung *to* that consolation as his suffering increased;
didn't want to cruelly suffer, *nor* want to be deceased.

For years he held the thought at bay, to seek a quick release
from physical-existence, when suffering should cease.
He knew he would need help in that, not easy to obtain,
due to politicians' power to perpetuate his pain,

based on their flawed perception, human-life must be retained,
regardless of cruel-suffering, so needlessly sustained,
perception that clouds concepts on which our faith relies—
especially that the soul survives our physical-demise.

On every level, it makes sense to have right laws in place,
aimed at relieving suffering that plagues the human-race,
to offer euthanasia to those pleading for release
from crushing pain-and-suffering set only to increase,

so long as that includes the right of sufferers to choose,
who, in their *own* assessment, just have nothing left to lose.
For them, and for their families, perhaps the *one* way-out,
from obscene burdens to be borne, escape nowhere-about.

They argue that such laws will open floodgates of abuse
and pressure on the old to die, with law as an 'excuse';
but, for millions, life is anguish, long before relief arrives,
collectively, that far outweighs 'concerns' for other lives.

It's *not* about the social-costs euthanasia could save,
nor many social-aspects eased or problems made less grave.
It *is* about *compassion*, serving first those suffering most,
and ameliorating misery in our country, coast-to-coast.

Winter Wine

I've woken in my bed's embrace
to wallow in a mental-drift;
winter hovers round my space,
embedded body's loathe to lift.

Extended arm seeks out a switch
and bedside-heater stirs to life;
this torso has no need to twitch,
caressed by comfort, free from strife.

Now notion of a need to rise,
subdued, suppressed and held at bay,
blocked by heavy, closing eyes,
departs my mind, denies dismay.

Seductive sleep seeks to ensnare
and draw me back into its hold,
and keep me there without a care,
defying winter, freed from cold.

I'm half-aware I must resist
surrender to this beckoning bed;
some inner-niggle does persist
to urge I stay awake instead.

Before I'm in too deep a dive,
with surface in too fast retreat;
against which plunge I must now strive
to *re*-claim consciousness-complete.

Some *re*call penetrates at last,
for work I'm seemingly so late;
bedcovers now aside are cast
in scrambling rush to defy Fate.

In stumbling panic, somehow dress,
with water-splash to eyes and face;
a rumbling stomach in distress,
that *wine* remembered with disgrace.

Now *only* when I've closed the door,
key left inside, can now just pray,
full memory reaches to restore:
Today's a public-holiday!

Don't Walk Away

Somehow our love seems to have stalled,
split from its precious space, well-walled,
inviting aspects to intrude,
no longer simple to exclude.

I could observe, but not define,
impacts of possible decline
that somehow probed the bond, to urge
some submerged self then to emerge.

Before, we seemed to blend as one
as surely as the sun had shone,
but time imposed some steady drip,
the cover of the bond to strip.

We clung so fiercely at first,
stayed in-each-other so immersed.
I ached with longing when apart;
she weighed, like pain, upon my heart.

Such yearning that should never lapse,
a force too sturdy to collapse.
There seemed no threat; there was no rift.
What set intensity adrift?

Yet, by degrees, it seemed to wane,
subdued emotion, less insane,
and more mature, as perceived,
and more secure, I believed.

We were united as a pair,
as all around were well aware,
and love was steady and entrenched;
could not be sidelined nor retrenched.

Or so I thought; I could relax,
indulge in sport, complain of tax,
booze with the boys and share crude jokes,
and never envy other blokes.

But now my heart will wither as you walk away from me.
For how long did I look at you through eyes that did not see?
And now I'm in some trance-state as I shed another tear.
Will I ever learn to love again, and do so free from fear?

Aspects of Ageing

I've changed my route to walking in an unfamiliar street.
I should focus on the surface and on lifting up my feet,
but my thought-flow has diverted to indulge in other things
by some automatic drifting that the human process brings.

A poised, protruding pavement-piece, predictably produced,
to trap my toe, disrupt me, as alarm is introduced.
The sense of falling fills me with a surging swell of dread
as impetus demands the pavement smack my face and head.

One outstretched hand does little to, at least, reduce the force.
My focus fights to fix upon this body's best resource.
In daze, I struggle to my knees, and find my feet again.
I need to blot out bleeding and combat oppressive pain.

This less-walked side-street spares my problem little heed.
I'm left alone to battle on, to stumble and to bleed.
I know all this will scarcely rate with sufferers, world-wide;
no impact on that suffering-scale from which we want to hide.

For most of us there comes a time when ageing takes its toll;
the body and the brain decline, assert decreased control.
Defensive measures are imposed by most of us, it seems,
increasingly to be absorbed by memories and dreams.

An option is embracing risk to wrestle time still left;
expand by such defiance *or* be broken and bereft;
so, is it best to battle, or adopt the brakes of age?
We need a window to our soul, or wisdom of a sage.

It seems our brains and bodies have agendas of their own;
advantages need not be earned, or suffering self-grown.
So much depends upon our birth, by luck or by design,
so, are we meant to self-promote, or to our 'fate' resign?

I can't relate to suffering, or reward it may bestow,
or even if it may provide a means by which to grow.
If I'm a human-being who is harbouring a soul,
I'll simply do the best I can and hope that makes me whole.

A stance I hope can 'take the strain', including growing old,
with due regard for each new day; need not be brashly bold.
Include degree of caution to keep suffering at bay,
and hope that proves sufficient at the end of that last day.

The Bridge

I brace myself to cross the bridge
outreaching from the rocky ridge
on which I pause, as though in plight,
perhaps impaired by fear or flight.

Should I proceed with strong resolve,
not knowing what that may involve;
but blessings to all left behind
and may this way to all be kind?

But is this structure safe and sound
to take me on to firmer ground,
or will it sag beneath my weight,
or sway to send me to my fate?

Beyond the bridge I cannot see.
Will it entrap or set me free?
For cloud obscures clear sight;
leaves little known of length or height.

How am I here, on some cliff
engulfed in silence, still and stiff;
and by what means did I arrive
somehow suspended, yet alive?
*

Confronted by a bridge to cross,
concerned, confused and at-a-loss?
Alertness makes no sudden surge,
but still some instinct or some urge,

compelling me to move ahead,
to trust this bridge on which to tread;
permitting faith to forge my way
as cloud disperses to display

such light, elusive to observe,
in which to steep and to preserve,
and to submerge and to restore
the essence of what went before;

and ponder not what lies ahead;
surrender to the light instead.
Embrace the bridge with steady stride,
and *love*, to reach the other side.

www.ingramcontent.com/pod-product-compliance
Lightning Source LLC
Chambersburg PA
CBHW030040100526
44590CB00011B/281